SMALLEY RELATIONSHIP
CENTER PRESENTS

secrets to
lasting love

journey to
a deeper relationship

name   date

©2003

SMALLEY RELATIONSHIP CENTER

1482 LAKESHORE DRIVE, BRANSON, MO 65616

417-335-4321   www.smalleyonline.com

isbn 0-9676732-1-6

CONGRATULATIONS! You are about to start an exciting adventure, an adventure that will challenge your relationship with your spouse and others. Everyone wants great relationships but not everyone is willing to take the steps to get there. This new video series will give you some practical, proven tools to start you on your journey.

It's exciting to see what is happening in the marriage and family area. For example, there are now over 100 major cities in the USA that have organized all of the priests, clergy, rabbis and some judges to sign a covenant that they will not marry a couple without learning relationship skills that prevent divorce and provide for a satisfying marriage.

Furthermore, there is a variety of research being conducted whose results are revealing some very specific ways to develop a great marriage. But even more important, the research is demonstrating that there are only four main ways to ruin a marriage. We call these four risk patterns, "relational germs." The three relational skills found within the "Secrets To Lasting Love" video series can actually act as "antibiotics" that eliminate these four "germs" in marriages. It has been scientifically proven that divorce can be reduced and these skills more than double your chances of staying in love... starting today.

- Read the notes before each session
- Take your own notes as you view the tape
- Go through the discussion questions after each session

We hope you will practice what you learn in this series. It will change your life. Your marriage relationship will grow deeper. All of us need ways to improve in every area of our lives, especially in our relationships.

At the end of each session, we have provided additional resources that deal with the session content. You can order most of these materials by visiting our web site (www.smalleyonline.com) or by calling 800-84-today.

The staff at Smalley Relationship Center have worked hard to see that you have an enjoyable and rewarding experience. At the end of this manual, we ask that you complete a "video evaluation" to help us improve the "Secrets To Lasting Love" video series.

We sincerely trust that this experience will be everything you hoped for...and more! Thank you for taking the time to invest in your most important relationships.

Yours for richer relationships,

Dr. Gary Smalley   Dr. Greg Smalley   Michael Smalley, M.A.

TABLE OF CONTENTS

INTRODUCTION

Did you know that the major cause of divorce is an inability to argue properly? Argument is like fire. It can cook your food or burn your house down. You have to learn how to harness it properly, or it will tear you and your mate apart. Reaching these deepest levels of intimacy takes more than hard work and a willingness to delve deep: it takes a set of three simple, yet astonishing skills that each and every successful relationship shares. These three skills represent all of my (Gary) thirty years of study, experience and counseling and have been tested in countless relationships. These skills, if properly and consistently practiced, have the ability to rocket your relationship to the deepest levels of intimacy.

These three skills are very powerful, and we've discovered that most couples only need these three to propel themselves into the deeper levels. There are more skills in the relationship arena, but like most couples, you may find that you only need these to maintain a happy and fulfilling relationship. They are the basic foundations to optimal relationships and your best defense against divorce.

#1. The Skill of Honor. This is the lighthouse, the beacon, the mighty rock on which every fulfilling relationship is built and every shaky relationship destroyed. When an adequate amount of honor is present in a relationship, a couple can withstand the roughest storms. When honor has been destroyed in a relationship, the couple is destined for disaster.

#2. The Skill of LUV Talk. This is the most honoring communication skill we know of! And it's a powerful ingredient to every fulfilling relationship. But we're not talking about simply communicating; we're talking about the most powerful communication method known to mankind: LUV Talk. This method will allow you and your mate to feel listened to, understood and validated–especially in times of conflict.

#3. The Skill of Constantly Recharging Your Mate's Needs Battery Through Love. Human beings have an "internal needs battery," and our actions produce either positive or negative "charges" to our mate's battery. Loving attention given to each other's needs undoubtedly has a positive effect. Selfish, negative, draining charges have a negative effect. It's been determined that couples literally throw thousands of positive and negative charges at each other in a typical day of interaction. We'll share the top seven relationship needs with you and show you how to discover your own needs, as well as your mate's needs, so you can begin the process of meeting those needs and regularly "recharging" each other.

The three skills may seem simple, but do not let this deceive you! Couples can't spend every moment in exercises and analysis. The daily process of living tends to grind us down, pushing us to compromise, to accept instead of choose what's best for our relationship. But there is always time for a reevaluation and reawakening. And when you're talking about the most important union in your life, could there be any better time but now?

MOVING FORWARD *(homework)*

Take the following test before the first Secrets To Lasting Love video.

In order to gain a realistic picture of your relationship, please answer each of the following questions in terms of your relationship with your 'mate' if married, or your 'partner' if dating or engaged. Use the following three point scale to rate how often you and your mate or partner experience the following:

1 = almost never   2 = once in a while   3 = frequently

____ Little arguments escalate into ugly fights with accusations, criticisms, name calling, or bringing up past hurts.

____ My partner criticizes or belittles my opinions, feelings, or desires.

____ My partner seems to view my words or actions more negatively than I mean them to be.

____ When we have a problem to solve, it is like we are on opposite teams.

____ I hold back from telling my partner what I really think and feel.

____ I think seriously about what it would be like to date or marry someone else.

____ I feel lonely in this relationship.

____ When we argue, one of us withdraws...that is, doesn't want to talk about it anymore; or leaves the scene.

_____ **TOTAL**

RELATIONSHIP DYNAMICS SCALE by Dr. Howard Markman & Dr. Scott Stanley. Used by permission.

The five Levels of intimate communication

SESSION AIM

This session is designed to help you understand the five levels of intimate communication that all couples desire to enter into during their marriage. Our specific goals in this session are to:

1. Identify the five levels of intimate communication

2. Explain why most relationships only exist on the first three levels

3. Identify the four relational germs that can destroy a relationship

4. Provide an overview of the three greatest relationship skills

WARM-UP *(pre-video discussion)*

1. What percent of the time do you typically communicate at the following five levels of intimate communication?

___Cliché Level ("It was sure hot today, wasn't it?")

___Fact Level ("How are you doing?")

___Opinions, Concerns or Expectations Level ("You're wrong and you know it.")

___Feelings Level ("Tell me if this is right; you feel afraid for our daughter because she is getting her driver's license.")

___Needs Level ("Are you saying you need more tenderness when we talk? Describe tenderness. What does it look like to you?")

_____

100% Total

2. What issues do you typically experience conflict over?

1 = Never   2 = Infrequent   3 = Sometimes   4 = Frequently   5 = Very Frequently

___Handling family finances   ___Sex relations

___Matters of recreation   ___Conventionality (right, good or proper conduct)

___Demonstration of affection   ___Philosophy of life

___Friends   ___Ways of dealing with in-laws

___Communication   ___Spirituality

VIDEO *(57 minutes of viewing)*

In the 18th Century, surgeons finally realized that post-operative infection was killing patients because they were using unsterilized instruments. The same kind of insight is available today within our "infected" marriages. The divorce epidemic is infecting our nation and world because of four main "germs." Furthermore, the marriage experts know how to "sterilize" a couple before and after marriage to prevent divorce. Like the positive transformation in surgery, we now realize that marriages could be dramatically more satisfying for couples. We are on the threshold of reducing the divorce rate and enhancing marriages around the world.

There are five levels of intimate communication that all happily married couples both desire to enter and do enter every day. The fourth and fifth levels of intimacy are the most satisfying and enriching part of marriage. Deep friendship can develop at the fourth and fifth levels. However, 50% of American couples can stagnate at the third level and consequently, can be "infected" with one or all of the four main "relationship germs" that cause divorce. Furthermore, of the 50% who remain married, only 25% are in satisfying relationships. Just as with post-surgical infection, we can no longer tolerate the condition of our marital relationships.

We have been trained by several marriage and family experts to understand not only what the "relational germs" are but the main skills that help couples enjoy a loving and lasting marriage. These four main "risk germs" usually occur at the third level of intimacy during arguments and can block couples from reaching those two deeper levels of intimacy. The weakest level of intimacy or closeness a couple can experience is when there is continual unresolved hurt, frustration or fear within their relationship. In order to fight the divorce patterns, we have developed three powerful skills that allow couples to enter the fourth and fifth levels of intimacy, simultaneously eliminating all four divorce risk patterns. The good news is that when couples use these three skills, they take control of their marriage and

enter into the deepest levels of love together. We have found that long-term, loving marriages have applied these three skills in their relationships in various degrees.

Let's look at the five levels of intimate communication:

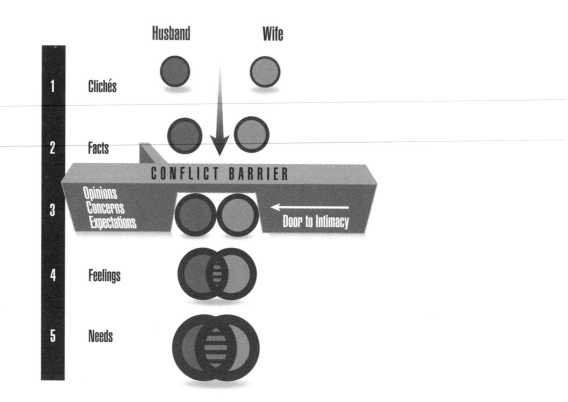

OVERVIEW OF THE FIVE LEVELS OF INTIMACY

THE FIRST LEVEL

Here, a couple simply tries to avoid each other and when they do speak, it is usually shallow conversation or exchanging cliches. They say things like:
> "How are you doing?"
> "I'm fine."
> "Please pass the salt."

At this level, there is little discussion about life or each other.

THE SECOND LEVEL

Here, the couple is sharing basic facts about themselves or life in general. At this point, there is little risk in starting an argument. They say things like:
> "It was sure hot today, wasn't it?"

"Can you believe what the President did today!"
A couple tends to avoid "facts" that could lead to conflict.

THE THIRD LEVEL

Here, the couple is at a greater risk in starting an argument. At this level, they can share their opinions, concerns or expectations.

"You never listen to me."

"You're wrong and you know it."

"If I had known how stubborn you are, we wouldn't be married."

It's at this point that an argument can ensue. If the couple has not learned how to handle arguments at this level, they are at risk for becoming infected with one or all of the four relational "germs." (The four "germs" are covered on pages 5 &6).

THE FOURTH LEVEL

The fourth level is achieved when a couple feels safe to share their deepest feelings and they treat each other's feelings as very valuable. When one mate asks the other about his or her concerns, opinions or an expectation, the one sharing is open, honest and responsible for his or her own feelings. They say things like:

"Tell me if this is right, you feel afraid for our daughter because she is getting her driver's license."

"It's not that you mind me watching TV, it's that you feel cheated that we don't spend more time together."

"I could be way off, but I feel sad when my parents don't come by and see us like they used to."

There is an atmosphere of honor, that is, the listener is trying to understand and validate what is being communicated. When we share our feelings, it is a person's attempt to express his or her deepest needs. Conflicts usually reveal that a person's feelings and needs are not being understood, validated or fulfilled.

THE FIFTH LEVEL

Level five is different than previous levels because this is where a person feels safe to share his or her own deepest needs. Safety is of the utmost importance. Also, when a mate shares his or her deepest relational needs, there is a feeling that those needs will be understood and valued. They usually say things like:

"See if this is right. You need some alone time at night after work and it's not that you don't want time with me, it's that you need to recoup?"

"Are you saying you need more tenderness when we talk? Describe tenderness. What does it look like to you?"

"Wait a minute, I don't understand. Am I getting this right? You're saying that we need to be saving more each month? What does that mean to you?" Since feelings reflect whether a person's needs are being met, a couple can honor each other as they move through the fourth level (feelings) into the fifth level (needs). For example, if a person has a need to be treated with tenderness, one might see expressions of frustration or hurt on the face of the offended person. Honor, at the fifth level of intimacy, would involve asking the offended person to share what is needed. If an environment of safety was established, he or she could express the need for more tenderness. The feelings of hurt, frustration or fear are reflections of a person's deeper need for tenderness. The seven most common relational needs are addressed in the third skill.

In conflicts or arguments, a couple can either move toward deeper intimacy or move toward the four relational "germs."

THE FOUR RELATIONAL GERMS

Dr. Howard Markman and Dr. Scott Stanley have discovered through over 20 years of research that there are four main risk factors (germs) that can lead to divorce. In their excellent book, *Fighting For Your Marriage*, they share that we greatly increase our chances of staying in love and in harmony if we avoid these four negative patterns. Here are the four main "germs" that can produce too much anger and possibly lead to divorce:

1. Withdrawal during an argument. Here one mate closes the other person out after an argument starts. For example, statements like:

> "I'm not talking about that any more, it's too hurtful."
> "I'll just leave the house if you continue talking about this. End of discussion; it's over."
> "That subject is not open for discussion."

2. Escalating during an argument. Here, the argument can get ugly. Escalation is when a person starts defending or trying to win an argument. Here, he or she volleys back and forth with shame and defensive statements. For example, shouting, blaming each other, using degrading names directed at your mate and trying to win the argument instead of cooperating as a team to solve the disagreement. Statements like the following might be used during escalation:

> "Don't you ever accuse me of that again!"
> "It's your fault that he talks to me like that, you're a great example!"
> "Forget it then. Go out with your friends, see if I care! Stay out all night, you like them better than me anyway."

There is usually an over use of the word "you" in an accusatory manner.

3. Belittling each other during an argument. Here, one mate accuses the other of being "dumb" or "stupid" in their thinking or feelings. Somehow, one mate is trying to belittle the other and prove that he or she is better than the other. This is the most destructive potential divorce risk pattern. It is also the opposite choice of honor.

> "That's the dumbest statement I have ever heard."
>
> "When will you ever get it right?"
>
> "You've been thinking from the wrong part of your body."

4. Having exaggerated or **false beliefs** about your mate during an argument. Here, one mate may believe that the other is trying to ruin or weaken the marriage on purpose.

> "You're always including your family. They've been between us our whole married life!"
>
> "You don't see it do you? You're too negative and it's driving me away!"
>
> "You say you're sorry, but you keep doing the same mean things over and over. You'll never change!"

The major problem with this fourth germ is that what humans believe about another, they tend to see and hear even if it isn't true. In other words, what you believe about another person (positive or negative), you will find evidence of that belief in everything he or she does or says.

GOING DEEPER *(intimate sharing)*

1. In the introduction section, you took the RELATIONSHIP DYNAMICS SCALE by Dr. Howard Markman & Dr. Scott Stanley. Markman & Stanley devised these questions based on 15 years of research at the University of Denver on the kinds of communication and conflict management patterns that predict if a relationship is headed for trouble. They have recently completed a nationwide, random phone survey using these questions. The average score was 11 on this scale, and higher scores mean your relationship may be in greater danger. What was your score on the Relationship Dynamics Scale?

8 to 12   "Green Light"

Now, if you scored in the 8-12 range, your relationship is probably in good or even great shape AT THIS TIME, but we emphasize, "AT THIS TIME," because relationships don't stand still. In the next 12 months, you'll either have a stronger, happier relationship, or you could head the other direction.

To think about it in another way, it's like you are traveling along and have come to a green light. There is no need to stop, but it is probably a great time to work on making your relationship all it can be.

13 to 17   "Yellow Light"

If you scored in the 13-17 range, it's like you are coming to a "yellow light." You need to be cautious. While you may be happy now in your relationship, your score reveals warning signs of patterns you don't want to let get worse. You'll want to be taking action to protect and improve what you have. Spending time to strengthen your relationship now could be the best thing you could do for your future together.

18 to 24   "Red Light"

Finally, if you scored in the 18-24 range, it's like approaching a red light. Stop and consider where the two of you are headed. Your score indicates the presence of "germs" that could put your relationship at significant risk. You may be heading for trouble or already be there.

But there is GOOD NEWS. No matter how you scored on the quiz, you can stop and learn ways to improve your relationship now! We encourage you to make a commitment to discover the "antibiotic" to deepen the relationship with your mate by using the three skills in this study guide!

2. How do you feel about your score on the Relationship Dynamics Scale? Remember, it's not where you fall (green, yellow or red light) but what you choose to do about it in the future that matters.

3. In which of these five levels do you spend most of your conversational time? Why is that?

4. Are you usually the first to go deeper to level four or five in communication, or does your partner usually initiate the sharing of feelings and needs? Why do you suppose that is?

5. Where are you within the five levels currently? Where do you operate now?

6. Give examples in your own relationship of the five levels. (e.g., How do you use cliches, facts, etc.)

7. Where do you want to operate? What would that look like within your relationship?

8. What do you need from your mate to get into the fourth and fifth levels of intimate communication?

1. *Making Love Last Forever* book-Dr. Gary Smalley
2. *Bound By Honor* book-Dr. Gary Smalley & Dr. Greg Smalley
3. *Fighting For Your Marriage* book-Markman & Stanley
4. *A Lasting Promise* book-Dr. Scott Stanley & others

MOVING FORWARD *(homework)*

1. Make a commitment to get into deeper levels.

2. Carefully record in the space below what your mate needs from you to get into the fourth and fifth levels of intimate communication.

_____

_____

_____

_____

_____

_____

_____

3. Note: Please complete the personality inventory on page 10 prior to the next video.

your mate's personality can improve your marriage

SESSION AIM

This session is designed to help you understand the concept of "color" and how we tend to marry someone whose color is much different than our own. Our specific goals in this session are to:

1. Explain what "color" means in a relationship

2. Identify your own personality color

3. Honor the strengths of each personality color

4. Show that when our strengths get pushed out of balance they can become some of our greatest weaknesses

5. Explain--based on personality color--how we tend to communicate, what we need and what balance looks like.

WARM-UP   *(pre-video discussion)*

1. Your homework for this session was to take the personality inventory. If you have not done so, please complete the test on page 10 at this time. Otherwise, graph your scores on page 11.

PERSONALITY PROFILE

In the space provided, identify the degree in which the following characteristics or behaviors most accurately describes you at home or in the relationships with your loved ones.
0 = not at all; 1 = somewhat; 2 = mostly; 3 = very much

I	II	III	IV
__ Likes control	__ Enthusiastic	__ Sensitive	__ Consistent
__ Confident	__ Visionary	__ Calm	__ Reserved
__ Firm	__ Energetic	__ Non-demanding	__ Practical
__ Likes challenge	__ Promoter	__ Enjoys routine	__ Factual
__ Problem solver	__ Mixes easily	__ Relational	__ Perfectionistic
__ Bold	__ Fun-loving	__ Adaptable	__ Detailed
__ Goal driven	__ Spontaneous	__ Thoughtful	__ Inquisitive
__ Strong willed	__ Likes new ideas	__ Patient	__ Persistent
__ Self-reliant	__ Optimistic	__ Good listener	__ Logical
__ Persistent	__ Takes risks	__ Loyal	__ Accurate
__ Takes charge	__ Motivator	__ Even-keeled	__ Controlled
__ Determined	__ Very verbal	__ Gives in	__ Predictable
__ Enterprising	__ Friendly	__ Indecisive	__ Orderly
__ Competitive	__ Popular	__ Dislikes change	__ Conscientious
__ Productive	__ Enjoys variety	__ Dry humor	__ Discerning
__ Purposeful	__ Group oriented	__ Sympathetic	__ Analytical
__ Adventurous	__ Initiator	__ Nurturing	__ Precise
__ Independent	__ Inspirational	__ Tolerant	__ Scheduled
__ Action oriented	__ Likes change	__ Peace maker	__ Deliberate
___ Total	___ Total	___ Total	___ Total

On the following page, record the totals on the appropriate graph space.

PERSONALITY PROFILE

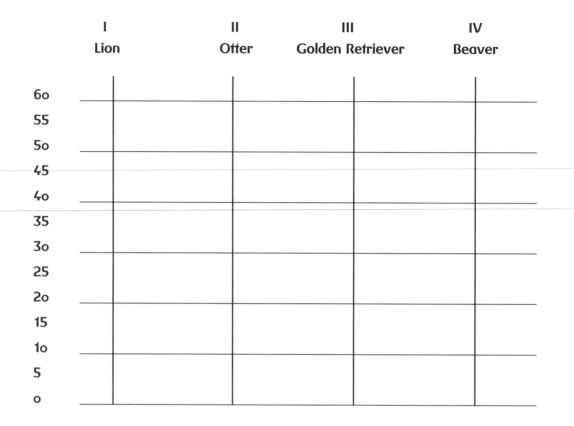

	I Lion	II Otter	III Golden Retriever	IV Beaver
60				
55				
50				
45				
40				
35				
30				
25				
20				
15				
10				
5				
0				

<u>**VIDEO**</u> *(50 minutes of viewing)*

When a man and a woman marry, they attempt to blend two different "colors." A person's color includes things like gender and personality differences, family of origin issues and societal norms. In order to gain a deeper understanding of each other's unique "color" we want to focus on personality differences and how they impact your relationship.

The personality inventory you take is not a test you fail or pass. It's more like a fingerprint that shows your tendencies. Tendencies can change, unlike fingerprints. Discovering your personality tendencies in relationships helps to show where your strengths and weaknesses exist.

Each of us has these personality strengths in combinations which are variable and adjustable. They need to be brought into balance. Therefore, the goal of this session is to honor your personality strengths and help you understand where you are "out of balance" in terms of your personality. We've found that our greatest personal strengths--when pushed out of balance--become our greatest weakness. For instance, let's say that your strength is tremendous enthusiasm; this becomes a weakness as your enthusiasm turns into manipulation or obnoxious behavior.

If a particular character trait of yours is too extreme, to the point that it irritates your mate or your children, you can decide to decrease that trait and increase the characteristics of other traits.

Let's take a closer look at four different personality (color) types to bring oneness, satisfaction and harmony to your relationship.

" L" IS FOR LION

Strengths	Strengths Pushed Out of Balance
* Problem solver	* Too busy
* Bold, direct communication	* Insensitive
* Decision maker	* Unthoughtful of others' wishes
* Strong willed	* Stubborn
* Independent, self-reliant	* Avoids people and seeking help
* Action oriented, persistent	* Inflexible, relentless, unyielding
* Likes authority	* Too direct or demanding
* Takes charge	* Pushy, impatient—do it now!
* Confident	* Cocky, overlooks feelings
* Enterprising	* Big risks
* Competitive	* Cold-blooded

Lions tend to have direct or blunt communication within a relationship. It is usually one-way so they can make poor listeners. In a relationship, Lions need such things as personal attention and recognition for what they do, areas where he or she can be in charge, opportunity to solve problems, freedom to change and challenging activities within a relationship.

What does a balanced Lion look like? Since Lions are naturally hard on problems, their greatest relational need is to add softness to their natural style to keep from being too hard on people in the process. Also, Lions may need to learn that meaningful communication takes time. They need to slow down and discuss decisions with others, not simply charge ahead on their own.

" O" IS FOR OTTER

Strengths	Strengths Pushed Out of Balance
* Enthusiastic	* Overbearing
* Takes risks	* Dangerous and foolish
* Visionary, inspirational	* Day-dreamer, phony
* Fun loving, infectious laughter	* Not serious, obnoxious
* Motivator, promoter, initiator	* Manipulator, exaggerates, pushy
* Energetic	* Impatient
* Friendly, group oriented	* Shallow relationships, bored
* Likes variety, enjoys change	* Scattered, lacks follow-through
* Spontaneous	* Not focused enough
* Enjoys creativity or new ideas	* Unrealistic, avoids details

Otters can inspire others through their communication. They tend to be optimistic or enthusiastic in their communication with others. It is usually one-way and their high energy can manipulate or wear others out. In a relationship, Otters need such things as approval, opportunity to verbalize, visibility and social recognition within a relationship.

What does a balanced Otter look like? One of the greatest relational needs for Otters is to be more of a follow-through person. Otters tend to make all kinds of promises and think "all things are possible," but they need to follow through with their commitments. Also Otters need to develop sensitivity to the feelings of others and weighing the consequences of their words or actions before jumping into something.

"G" IS FOR GOLDEN RETRIEVER

Strengths	Strengths Pushed Out of Balance
✱ Sensitive feelings	✱ Easily hurt
✱ Loyal	✱ Misses opportunities
✱ Calm, even-keeled	✱ Lacks enthusiasm
✱ Non-demanding, patient	✱ Push-over, taken advantage of
✱ Peace maker, hates confrontation	✱ Misses honest intimacy
✱ Enjoys routine, dislikes change	✱ Stays in rut, not spontaneous
✱ Warm & relational	✱ Fewer deep friends
✱ Accomodating	✱ Too indecisive
✱ Sympathetic, good listener	✱ Holds on to other's hurt or pain

A Golden Retriever's communication style tends to be more indirect. They usually have good two-way communication with others; thus, make great listeners. However, they tend to use too many words or provide too many details. In a relationship, Golden Retrievers need such things as emotional security and an agreeable environment within a relationship.

What does a balanced Golden Retriever look like? Since Golden Retrievers have an eagerness to please others, they have a hard time saying "No." Therefore, their greatest relational need is to set limits and boundaries essential for their own well-being. Further, Retrievers need to practice confronting others. Turn your ability to feel deeply about negative things into a positive step, one where you think and act decisively.

"B" IS FOR BEAVERS

Strengths	Strengths Pushed Out of Balance
✱ Perfectionist	✱ Too controlling
✱ Detailed, enjoys instructions	✱ Hard time finishing, slow
✱ Accurate, precise	✱ Too critical and too strict
✱ Consistent, predictable	✱ No spontaneity or variety, boring
✱ Controlled, reserved, orderly	✱ Too serious and stuffy, rigid
✱ Practical	✱ Not adventurous
✱ Sensitive	✱ Stubborn
✱ Conscientious	✱ Too inflexible
✱ Analytical	✱ Loose overview
✱ Discerning	✱ Too negative of new opportunity

Beavers tend to be factual and precise in their communication with others. They usually have good two-way communication with others and also make good listeners–especially in relation to tasks. However, their desire for detail and precision can frustrate others. In a relationship, Beavers need such things as quality and exact expectations within a relationship.

What does a balanced Beaver look like? Since Beavers tend to be extreme in their thinking, it's important for them to realize that nothing is ever as bad as it seems or as good as it appears. Stop catastrophizing. Instead, be more relaxed and let some things remain unfinished or undone. Letting go of the need to have everything exactly right is important for a Beaver. They, too, can learn to turn negatives in their life into a positive, instead of magnifying a mess all out of proportion into something really bad.

We trust you'll share this inventory with your mate, friends and your kids. By understanding your personality bent and how your weaknesses are really your strengths pushed out of balance, then you will have fewer personality conflicts down the road.

SUPPLEMENTARY RESOURCES

1. *The Two Sides of Love* book-Smalley & Trent
2. *Taming the Family Zoo* book-Jim and Suzette Brawner
3. *The Treasure Tree* book-Smalley & Trent
4. *The Two Trails* book-Dr. John Trent

GOING DEEPER *(intimate sharing)*

1. How do you feel about the results of taking the test? Do you agree with the results?

2. Which of your own personality strengths do you most honor or treasure?

3. How do these strengths benefit or enhance your marital relationship?

4. Summarize in your own words why it's important to know your personal balance point.

5. Describe a time when you said or did something you later regretted, and you realized the problem was that one of your strengths got pushed to an extreme.

6. How does understanding another person's personality bent help us relate better to that individual?

7. On the personality test your mate completed on page 10 of his or her manual, he or she identified several characteristics or behaviors that described him or her best. Read over the items that your mate ranked a "3" and list five of these characteristics that you admire in the following spaces.

My mate's personality strengths that I most honor and treasure include:

a. _____

b. _____

c. _____

d. _____

e. _____

8. How do these strengths benefit or enhance your marital relationship?

a. _____

b. _____

c. _____

d. _____

e. _____

9. What are some weak areas you would like to develop?

10. How do your spouse's strengths expose your weaknesses?

11. What qualities of other personality types would you like to develop? Why?

12. What can you do to affirm and complement your spouse's unique personality? How can you blend your strengths with your spouse?

13. Do you see where your weaknesses may hurt or irritate your spouse?

14. How will this personality knowledge be helpful in parenting?

15. Categories can be helpful and harmful. What do you think will be the positive benefits of knowing your personality type? Do you think there are any negatives?

MOVING FORWARD *(homework)*

Take some time this week to praise your family for their individual personality strengths.

skill one:
HONOR... The single greatest skill for a satisfying marriage

SESSION AIM

This session is designed to help you understand why honor is the foundation within a marriage that everything else is built upon. No matter how successful a couple is at mastering the other relational skills, without honor, the relationship is destined for destruction. Our specific goals in this session are to:

1. Explain what it means to "confer distinctive value upon someone"

2. Explain what it means to "decide that your mate's opinions, concerns and expectations are just a little more valuable than your own"

3. Provide three simple, yet powerful methods to make honor a viable part of your relationship.

WARM-UP *(pre-video discussion)*

Describe a time when you felt honored or valued by someone (a parent, spouse, coach, teacher, boss, co-worker or friend). How did the person indicate you were valued? How did that make you feel?

VIDEO *(55 minutes of viewing)*

Start the tape.

HONOR

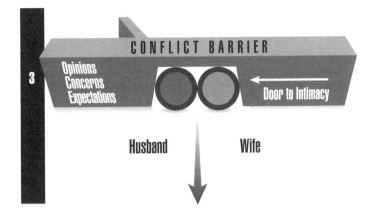

The best definition of honor that we've found involves two extremely important parts. First, honor is anytime we "confer distinctive value" upon someone. When a college bestows an honorary doctorate degree, the school is conferring distinction upon someone. When an audience applauds or an individual bows before someone, they are conferring distinction.

The second part of honor is deciding that your mate's opinions, concerns and expectations are just a little more valuable than your own. The highest level of love and maturity is when both husband and wife prefer the other's feelings and needs above his or her own. In other words, you choose to be a LUVR (Lover): With opinions, concerns and expectations, you decide to Listen, Understand, Value and Resolve the arguments with win-win solutions.

Honor does not involve the belief that your opinions, concerns and desires are somehow superior to your partner's. Conveying a superior attitude is the biggest killer of marriage and produces the most frustration, hurt and fear within marriage. Honor is a "lifting up," a holding up of your mate with reverence. It's the selfless process of proclamation: in honoring you are telling your mate that he or she is paramount in your life and his or her status in your hierarchy of values is above all petty arguments, disagreements and opinions. Honor is permanent, unmovable and forever.

Honor is the most important skill you can master; the others can't and won't work without honor. One marriage expert, Dr. John Gottman, says that without honor, all the marriage skills one can learn won't work. Another expert, Dr. Scott Stanley, says that honor is the fuel that keeps the life long marriage loving and functioning. If honor is non-existent in one partner, there is a high probability that the marriage is over. But if only a spark of respect or adoration remains, the spark can be turned into a flame in a few days.

THE DECISION TO HONOR YOUR MATE INVOLVES THREE SIMPLE STEPS

There are three steps to building honor in your relationship, erecting a firewall protecting you and your spouse from the storms that will certainly come along:

❋ Raise the value of your mate as high as possible. In other words, decide how much a person is worth. First, confer valuable distinction upon your mate. Next, choose to highly value your mate just a little above yourself. Imagine that your mate's smile is God's autograph.

❋ Increase the brightness of honor through observing your mate's best qualities. Then, make a list of all the positive characteristics and qualities of your mate. Your appreciation list will become points of value. The longer the list, the stronger the marriage.

❋ Shine your mate's "light" for others to see by praising your mate to others, and giving gifts to express your delight.

SUPPLEMENTARY RESOURCES

1. *Love is a Decision* book-Smalley & Trent
2. *Hidden Keys to a Loving & Lasting Relationships* book-Dr. Gary Smalley

GOING DEEPER *(intimate sharing)*

1. What could your mate do that would make you feel like he or she is "conferring distinction" upon you?

2. What could your mate do that would make you feel like he or she is "deciding that your opinions, concerns and expectations are just a little more valuable than his or her own?"

3. In the video, Gary taught that we can imagine that our mate's smile is God's autograph. Like God's autograph, what are some other valuable things you could imagine to express how valuable your mate is (e.g., diamond, billion dollar bill, etc.)?

4 . List five of your mate's qualities or character traits that you admire most.

a. _____

b. _____

c. _____

d. _____

e. _____

5 . From the list you created in question 4, pick your most favorite positive quality and share it with the group. What is it about that quality that makes it your favorite? In what ways does that quality enhance your marriage?

_____

_____

_____

_____

6 . Brainstorm with your mate and construct a list of the types of gifts you could give your mate to express your delight. Be sure to include things that do not cost money, are inexpensive, as well as his or her "wish" list items.

Your mate's gift list includes:

_____   _____

_____   _____

_____   _____

_____   _____

M O V I N G   F O R W A R D *(homework; "one-on-one," on your own time)*

In the future, we encourage you to expand the list you started in question 4. Make it as long as possible. Make a commitment to share these encouraging words with your mate as often as conceivable. Also, praise your mate to others and give gifts to express your delight.

skill Two: LUV TALK... The number one communication method in the world

SESSION AIM

This session is designed to help you understand how to use a powerful communication method that can instantly cause each other to feel listened to, understood and validated. Our specific goals in this session are to:

1. Explain what LUV Talk is and how we use it.

2. Explain how to use LUV Talk by giving you rules for the speaker and rules for the listener

3. Explain how to create a "Win / Win" solution

WARM-UP

What is your favorite fast food restaurant? When was the last time you ate there?

VIDEO *(55 minutes of viewing)*

Start the video.

LUV Talk

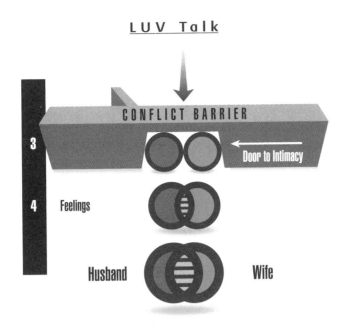

You have probably already practiced LUV Talk whether you realized it or not. Every time you pass through a drive-through window at your favorite fast-food restaurant, you've been engaged in LUV Talk. You place your order, then the drive-through attendant repeats your order back to you. Like the fast-food clerk repeats a customer's order, a mate using LUV Talk repeats what his or her mate has said. This communication method not only clarifies the conversation and prevents misunderstanding; it allows the couple to delve into the deeper meanings behind their words. Just imagine how many millions of dollars these fast food restaurants have spent to find the best communication method to stay "married" to their customers. We can use the same method for free to stay married to our mate. We're going to show you how.

This is a powerful communication method that allows each mate to be a "LUVR." When your mate feels **L**istened to, **U**nderstood and **V**alidated, then as a team you both can **R**esolve the conflict with a win-win solution. You will argue mainly about three things: opinions, concerns or expectations.

For example, a wife might say, "It's very frustrating and I feel fearful when you don't call me when you're going to be late. Or when you're on a trip and you don't let me know you've arrived and you are safe." She is taking responsibility for her own emotions; that is, she is explaining that she is frustrated and fearful. She needs to be heard, understood and validated for her feelings. Her husband's response is similar to what a fast-food customer would hear at a drive-through menu and speaker. After the customer's order is given, the restaurant employee usually repeats the order back.

In LUV Talk a couple follows the same basic actions that occur at the majority of fast-food restaurants. In this illustration, the wife first "places her feelings and needs order," then her husband acts like the employee. He repeats what he heard her order. "Let me see if I heard you. You are saying that it's very frustrating when I seem to ignore your feelings of fear when I don't call to let you know I am safe." She answers, "Yes, that's how I feel." Or she can make corrections to the order if he heard her incorrectly.

He then responds by thinking or saying, "So, that's who you are" (validation). He doesn't have to agree with her or change any of his behaviors, or feel it's somehow his fault that she is frustrated. That's just the way she chose to react to her circumstances. After she feels understood and validated, it's his turn to share his feelings or needs. Therefore, the couple reverses positions. Now the husband has a turn to respond to his wife's order or place his own order. She becomes the restaurant employee in order to listen and validate his feelings and needs. He might say, "I feel belittled in some ways, like I intend to hurt you when I forget to call." She responds by saying, "Let me see if I understand what you just said. You're saying you feel put down and shamed whenever I am upset about you not calling me." "That's right," he answers. Then she asks "Would you like anything else with your order?" That means, do you have any other feelings or needs you wish to share? It is only after they both feel understood and validated that they can resolve the argument by finding a "win-win" solution.

After using this powerful communication skill, the average couple is amazed at how easy it is to find a win-win solution. A win-win solution is finding a choice that is mutually desirable and acceptable to both parties involved.

It has been scientifically proven that if a couple can speak to each other with honor, understanding and validation during an argument, the four divorce "germs" are eliminated. However, there are very simple rules that must be followed when using "LUV Talk."

LUV Talk Rules

Employee	Customer
1. Listen	1. Talk for yourself
2. Understand	2. Bite-size phrases
3. Validate	3. Wait for astonishment
4. Blend	4. Win / Win solution

WARNING...

One word of caution, we highly encourage you not to begin LUV Talk on a highly sensitive subject or a very hurtful area from your past. Start with less volatile conflicts like being late for dinner or maybe your dream vacation. Difficult subjects like in-laws, money or sex can be troublesome at first. As your skills increase at using this life-changing method, you may feel safer to use it with more serious and sensitive matters. *Take your time.* It's not something you try and stop using because it didn't work like you wanted. Trust us, it works. It's been proven for years to be one of the most powerful communication methods available and it definitely lowers the anger level at home, at the office or at school.

"LUV Talk" in Action

To gain further understanding of this powerful communication method, it can be helpful to "see" it in action. A couple we know hit the "wall of conflict" one day as they were discussing Cheryl's tendency to be late. Scott was growing more frustrated by the month. They had been married for almost ten years and the problem was gaining momentum. They were both storing up greater amounts of anger. Scott had resorted to little sarcastic comments (escalation) if it looked as if Cheryl was running late. This would subsequently result in Cheryl not talking for long periods of time (withdrawal). If this pattern was allowed to continue, then they stood a great chance of weakening their relationship.

They first agreed to use LUV Talk. Watch how they reached a "Win / Win" solution to the conflict in minutes, without actually trying to do so.

Cheryl asked to be the "customer" first and Scott agreed to be the "employee." He began by saying, "Welcome to the Smith home, may I take your order?"

"I feel very frustrated by the pressure you put on me when I'm going as fast as I can," Cheryl said. Scott tried to repeat what he'd heard in his own words, "You feel frustrated because you're getting ready so slow and I put pressure on you." [This is why this communication method is so effective because it resolves miscommunication] "That not quite what I said," said Cheryl calmly, "I'm getting ready as fast as I can and I feel frustrated when you put pressure on me to go faster." "You feel frustrated when I try to get you moving faster as you're getting ready in the morning," repeated Scott. "That right!" agreed Cheryl.

Next, Scott asked Cheryl if she wanted anything else with her order. She continued, "I have so many things to do before we leave, I feel frustrated because I could use your help." Scott then repeated her words, "You feel frustrated because you could use my help to finish all the things you need done before leaving the house." After going back and forth, Cheryl explained that she felt understood and validated. [Again, Scott didn't have to "agree" with what Cheryl was saying; instead, his job was to honor and validate his wife's feelings.]

The couple then traded places and Cheryl began with the same invitation. "Welcome to the Smith home, may I take your order?" The funny part about this exercise is what happened next. Scott's first statement actually solved their problem. "I feel frustrated because I always get ready before you and then I just sit around waiting for you. It's boring," he articulated.

Cheryl smiled, and repeated his words slowly and lovingly. "If I hear you correctly, you get frustrated and bored just sitting around, waiting for me to finish getting ready."

"That's right," Scott said looking a little puzzled. Finally he put two and two together and realized why she was smiling. Cheryl needed help with several things before they were ready to leave the house. Instead of helping, he'd get bored by doing nothing.

At this point, Scott had nothing more to say; instead, he was ready to look for a "Win / Win" solution.

How to Find a "Win/Win" Solution

The goal for finding a workable and mutually satisfying solution is to discover one that those involved feel good about. We call this a win/win solution. The main rule for finding a win/win solution is not to finalize anything until both individuals in the argument have been heard, understood and feel valued by each other. Again, this is why you continue to use LUV Talk throughout the process.

After sharing and having your feelings and needs understood, many times, the solution is obvious. Sometimes it's not, however, apparent to everyone.

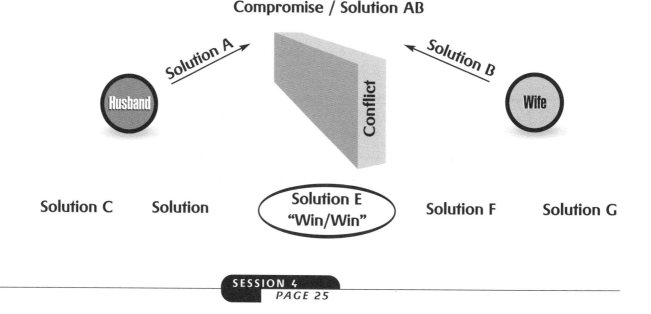

In the above diagram, we have illustrated how a win/win solution is developed. When two people get into an argument, usually they have their own solution to the problem (Solution A & Solution B). Sometimes they can agree to compromise (Solution AB), but here, no one really wins. It's like a half win because they both give in some. On the other hand, a win/win solution is when both individuals brainstorm several additional solutions (C-G) by letting them go like balloons up in the air. At first, you do not evaluate the possible solutions (C-G). After all ideas are "up in the air" then both individuals evaluate and determine if there is one solution that they both like (Solution E for example). This is different than a compromise because instead of both giving in, they find a different solution that is acceptable. They leave their original impasse (Solutions A & B), and find another answer that they both agree is the best solution to their problem. Thus, they reach a "win/win" resolution.

Returning to Scott and Cheryl's illustration, they began to brainstorm possible solutions. For example, Scott could help out instead of sitting around bored, and Cheryl could start getting ready earlier. They agreed that the combination of these two things would create a relational "win/win." Sometimes a "win/win" can be one or both of the original solutions (A and/or B). The main point is that both agree that the solution is the best choice—thus, it's a WIN for the relationship!

See how quickly a solution can appear once two people share their needs and feelings. Sometimes, however, we may not understand or even see an obvious solution. This is why when trying to determine the best solution for a problem, it still must be done in honor. Cheryl could have shamed Scott for not realizing that she needed help.

Sometimes, when you cannot decide upon a solution, you may need to go back and LUV Talk some more. If you remain persistent, most conflicts can be resolved.

Additional LUV Talk Demonstration

Conflict: *Terry and Janna built their house, finished the basement so it's like an apartment and discussed the possibility of using the apartment for guests, but terms were never decided upon. The frustration came from having too many guests, how do we decide which guests, and how often...*

Gary - Okay, we're going to use LUV Talk. Either one can start and I'll be the coach. Express your needs and feelings. For example, "I feel fearful; I feel lonely; I feel frustrated." Avoid using the word 'you'. This is just how you're feeling about this thing.

Janna - I like to be around people. I love being home, but sometimes after being home by myself all day, I get so excited when I think of people coming and us having people around.

Gary - Remember to say short phrases so he can repeat what he's hearing you say.

Terry - I'm hearing you say that you enjoy having people around because you don't have that during the day, and it's more fun for you to have more people around. Is that right?

Janna - And sometimes I feel apprehensive when I want to offer it to someone because I'm afraid of your response and that you'll be frustrated. I know it's important to have boundaries. I want to honor you because I know it's hard to work all day and come home to a lot of people.

Terry - You feel apprehensive about asking for someone to use the basement because you fear my response. You want to be able to offer it to them, but you also want to honor me.

Janna - I feel only certain people would be able to come. I feel like some people would be met with a negative response.

Terry - You feel that I'm not going to be excited about certain people staying here.

Janna - I don't know how to determine who you're going to be excited about. Sometimes you say you just need to warm up to the idea and once you're into it, you enjoy it. I don't know how to determine if it's going to be one of those situations or if it's something you just don't really want to do.

Terry - You're not sure how to decide which people I'm going to be excited about. But at the same time you know that sometimes I warm up to situations. So it makes you unsure of whether to even present the idea.

Janna - Right.

Gary - Now if Janna has expressed her feelings where she feels Terry understands, it is his turn.

Terry - I feel like our basement is part of our house. When I visualize our house, I visualize our home.

Janna - You visualize the basement as part of our home - not separate like some guest apartments would be.

Terry - It's my comfort zone, and I do get excited about people coming over, but if I had a stressful day at the office dealing with a lot of people, then it's fun to come home and have time with just you.

Janna - It's hard to be excited about coming home knowing that there are going to be other people here, if you've had lots of interaction with people all day long.   So you just want to be able to relax with me, which is nice.

Terry - I'm more of a one-on-one person as a golden retriever. I get the same amount of energy from one person (like my best friend) that you get from other people.

Gary - Express more of your feelings. Like "I feel frustrated to come home; I feel discouraged..."

Terry - I feel frustrated by not having a plan. It's not so much that I have a scheme of people that are good or bad, because with most people, once I understood it, I said, "Great. Yes."

Janna - So you need structure. It's harder for you to get excited no matter who it is if it's not planned out or if you don't know what to expect.

Terry - Right. I'm not frustrated if there is a plan that I have the energy for. But if someone unexpected is coming from Friday through Sunday, and I worked all week, then in my mind, I just shut down. I'm not going to have any recuperation time this weekend. My time is gone.

Janna - Then you can't prepare. When someone unexpected is going to be here all weekend, you don't know what to expect and that frustrates you because you don't know if that person is going to just be down in the basement the whole time or if they're going to be up here draining your energy. Then you won't have time to recoup.

Terry - I have a certain amount of emotional energy. I get energized and just enjoy being with you. But if there are five people here and they are all strangers, I want to be honoring and know we're going to have to chat. I want to, but I think we're going to be doing this until midnight.

Janna - That drains energy from you rather than giving you energy like it does for me, perhaps.

Gary - But at the same time, you give him energy.

Janna - But one-on-one time with me or a good friend would really give you energy.

Terry - That's it.

Gary - Do you both understand each other? Sometimes I encourage couples to review with a quick summary. Give me a few sentences what you think she's feeling and what you think he's feeling.

Terry - It's frustrating for you to know whether the basement is really a guest place or not and who we allow to use it for that.

Gary - Maybe you need a different definition for your basement.

Janna - Your frustration comes from not having a plan or structure, which is really what I'm saying too. You just need to know ahead of time so you know what to expect. If you can expect it and work up to it, then it's like you put back a little energy to have for that time.

Terry - Exactly.

Gary - Now what we're going to do is fill helium balloons and put them on the table here and you're going to write on them with an imaginary marker various creative ideas. There is no wrong idea, because you don't evaluate any of the ideas. These are ideas for a solution. We're going to throw them up on the ceiling and they are going to stick on the ceiling. After you get as many as you want, then you'll pick one out that you both like. Either one of you throw out ideas.

Janna - Well, we talked about writing down or having something for guests down there for when they come, something that says 'Welcome to our house.'

Terry - One idea is to actually come up with how many people per month would be comfortable for both of us. So let's say it's twice a month, on the weekend, maximum. Something like that.

Janna - Also with that — something to establish structure for people just using it for the day or evening, but not spending the night.

Terry - The only thing that makes me fearful of a situation where it's a person that I don't know is that if there are no rules, the person doesn't have any ownership. What if someone brings their dog, or invites other friends? We need ground rules.

Janna - I don't tend to say that at first. I'm very agreeable. So they think they have more leeway than we want them to have. Then I get frustrated and he knows that. So he wants to help alleviate that.

Gary - Anything else?

Janna - We should just check up with each other periodically about how we're feeling about it.

Gary - Now, look at all the options and pick your favorite solution. You might want to pick a few. Find something you can agree on and both feel like you're going to win with.

Janna - I think both of us like the idea of having some structure, something written down for us as well as for our guests.

Gary - Would that do it for both of you?

Terry - Yes, except it would help me if I can picture a quantity of some kind. If she asked if she could invite two people over a week, if it came up, and then I'd say which we could pick.

Gary - In other words, you want to have all the aspects in writing. Think of everything you can, like what to do in emergencies. What does a normal month look like, and so on.

Janna - Or families. When I was on the phone with my brother-in-law one time and he said, "Yeah, I'm going to come down there." Of course, I felt that since he is my brother-in-law, I needed to offer the place to him. But I hadn't talked to Terry.

Gary - Well, you can include something about relatives that don't abuse this, you can say you have the freedom to say yes. That would be like an emergency thing, if you agree.

SUPPLEMENTARY RESOURCES
_____

1. *Bound By Honor* book-Dr. Gary Smalley & Dr. Greg Smalley
2. *A Lasting Promise* book-Dr. Scott Stanley
3. *Fighting for Your Marriage* book-Dr. Markman & Dr. Stanley

GOING DEEPER *(intimate sharing)*

1. If you need an additional example of LUV Talk in action, see page 39 (Terry and Jana).

2. What do you think about the LUV Talk method? Do you like the method? Why? Why not?

3. Do you see yourself using LUV Talk when you hit the wall of conflict?

4. See if you can list all eight of the LUV Talk rules for both the "employee" (listener) and the "customer" (speaker) (if you need help, see page 23):

Employee	Customer
1. **L** _____	1. **T** _____
2. **U** _____	2. **B** _____
3. **V** _____	3. **W** _____
4. **B** _____	4. **W** _____

5. Practice LUV Talk by answering the following three questions with one another. Remember to provide as many details as possible so you get the opportunity to practice repeating back their "order." One of you must agree to be the customer (speaker) and the other the employee (listener). The employee starts out by asking, "Welcome to the (your name) house, may I take your order?" Then the customer begins sharing either the date night, dream vacation or future dreams.

* What would your ideal date-night look like?
* What is your dream vacation?
* What are some of your dreams for the future both individually and as a couple?

6. Practice finding a "win/win" solution for question four. Based on each other's favorite date night activity, use the brainstorming process described in the video and on page 38 to discover a "win/win" solution.

First, list all the possible ideas you could do on your next date night:

_____

_____

_____

_____

_____

_____

Next, both of you choose your top choice. Place an asterisk next to the two choices.

Finally, see if you can agree on one choice. Circle the final choice.

Have fun!

MOVING FORWARD *(homework; on your own time)*

1 . We will go out on our ideal date on the following time and date: _____

2 . To get ready for session six, please answer the following question: "What is your most important relational need?"

_____

_____

_____

_____

_____

_____

SKILL THREE:
Discovering and Meeting the most important Relational needs of your mate

SESSION AIM

This session is designed to help you understand the top seven relational needs. Our specific goals in this session are to:

1. Identify the seven most important relational needs

2. Explain how to meet those needs in your mate

3. Help you generate your own top relational needs list

WARM-UP *(pre-video discussion)*

1. What is the value of meeting each other's relational needs?

2. How does it positively impact your marriage when you meet each other's relational needs?

VIDEO *(58 minutes of viewing)*

Start the video.

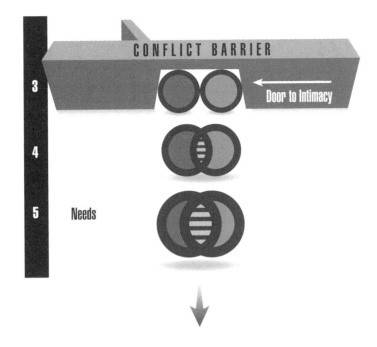

The fifth level of intimacy, the deepest level of communication, involves discovering the most important needs to be met in your relationship, and you can make a living plan to meet each other's needs. But to stay here, you and your mate must become masters of meeting your most important individual needs. Only in meeting these needs can you truly become one and remain in the deepest level of love.

Relational needs require constant attention! Misunderstood or unfulfilled needs can send your relationship ricocheting back to the superficial levels of intimacy, perhaps even hurtling out the door and toward the heartbreak of divorce. Our counseling office is filled with people who, not understanding, much less meeting, their mates' needs find themselves in deep trouble.

Our survey of relational needs, which has included thousands of couples, led to an interesting conclusion: *what most couples consider to be their top needs are the same needs that, unfulfilled, lead to the main causes of arguments described by the leading researchers in the relationship field.* What does this mean? When needs are not being met, look out! Your marriage is at stake. Your mate will become overly defensive, argumentative, jealous, belligerent, withdrawn or degrading of others. When our deepest relational needs are not met, we tend to be more irritated, discouraged, edgy, hypersensitive and reactionary to "average" events that occur in a typical marriage.

Furthermore, the need for companionship in a long-lasting relationship is so strong that men and women will go to any length to satisfy it. But if marriage isn't meeting their needs, they may go outside the marriage and into an emotional or sexual affair. Or these needs will be fulfilled at work, play, through relatives, friends, children or in the community at large.

THE SEVEN BASIC NEEDS: MEET THEM OR ELSE!

One thing is certain: before you can begin meeting your mate's deepest needs, you have to know what they are. The first law of fulfilling needs is to realize that everyone's are different, based on personalities, backgrounds and expectations. So you must first learn to recognize your mate's individual needs, as well as your own. Based on our research with couples, here are the top seven relational needs:

1. The need to feel my mate is being honest and trustworthy.

2. The need to feel a mutual commitment that we'll stay together and feel secure in love. This includes a working plan to resolve our personal problems or conflicts.

3. The need to feel that we're both maintaining a mutually vibrant spiritual relationship.

4. The need to feel accepted and valued for (a) who I am (my opinions, thoughts and beliefs) and (b) what I do.

5. The need to feel I'm being included in most decisions that affect (a) my life (because I want to become a "We," not just a "Me," as I was before marriage) or (b) the need to feel I'm being included in most decisions that affect my marriage (Who's the boss?).

6. The need to feel connected through (a) talking or (b) spending recreational time together as a couple.

7. The need to feel my mate is giving me (a) verbal or (b) physical tenderness.

Of course, all these needs mean different things to different people. It's important for you and your mate to go through the list thoroughly and create a mutual understanding of what these needs mean to you individually. Let your mate speak freely and openly about needs important to him or her. You might get to see an integral piece of your mate's heart. Let your mate determine the best ways to meet his or her needs. Do not try to read their minds. They know their needs best! Most importantly, use LUV Talk to understand their needs.

Recognizing your mate's needs is a critical first step, but the force that has the ability to consistently take you to the deepest levels of intimacy is the recharging of these needs on a daily basis.

RECHARGING YOUR MATE'S NEEDS DAILY

Imagine a seven-cell battery, each cell wired to one of your mate's top basic needs. Now, consider each of these needs as individual power cells in your mate's relational "battery." When the "battery cells" are drained by everyday living, working, children, friends and "just life in general," humans need their relational batteries recharged, just like your car battery needs charging after too much neglect or overuse.

What charges car batteries is electricity. What charges human relational batteries is attending to your partner's needs — and it only takes about twenty minutes a day! We learned the "twenty minute theory" from relationship expert Dr. John Gottman. He discovered through his research that the difference between a couple who divorces and one that stays together but unhappy is ten minutes a day of "turning towards" each other. By this, he means that a couple must "turn towards" each other every day through positive words or affirmative interactions.

Furthermore, Gottman found that couples who stay together and are happy "turn towards" each other an additional ten minutes more each day than unhappily married couples. From these discoveries we can surmise that a total of twenty minutes a day of "turning towards each other" in substantial ways can make the difference between divorce and staying together in a satisfying relationship.

To understand the current state of your mate's battery, look to their feelings. Feelings are a gauge of how needs are being met. Some of the feelings that will indicate a low battery include hurt, frustration and fear; conversely, indications of a fully charged battery include joy, happiness and ecstasy.

The human "needs" battery requires constant recharging. How do you do it? First you have to discover what your mate's needs are and then you spend at least twenty minutes per day "recharging" those needs.

SUPPLEMENTARY RESOURCES

1. *Hidden Keys to Loving and Lasting Relationships* video series-by Dr. Gary Smalley
2. *Making Love Last Forever* book-Dr. Gary Smalley
3. *Five Love Languages* book-Dr. Gary Chapman
4. *His Needs Her Needs* book-Dr. Willard Harley
5. *Seven Principles For Making Marriage Work* book-Dr. John Gottman

GOING DEEPER *(intimate sharing)*

1. Have you had any misunderstood or unfulfilled needs that sent your relationship ricocheting back to the superficial levels of intimacy? What were some? What did you do about this dilemma?

2. What happens in your relationship when important needs go unfulfilled? Do you get infected from any of the "germs?" Which one(s) (withdrawal, escalating, belittling, or false beliefs)?

3. On a scale of 1 - 10, with ten being completely secure; how secure do you feel in your relationship to share those needs?

Insecure								Completely Secure	
1	2	3	4	5	6	7	8	9	10

4. What do you need to feel secure and be willing to share your most important relational needs?

5. How can your mate draw out your most important relational needs?

6. Of the seven needs we covered in the video, which ones are top on your list? Which one is the most important need you have?

MOVING FORWARD

Since every couple is different, it's important to create your own "hierarchy of needs" by reviewing the following list of needs and then answering the ensuing questions.

A. In order to understand which of the following needs are the most important in your life, rank each one from zero to ten (ten being the most important). If there are any additional needs that are not on the list, write them into the "other needs" line.

____ 1. Feel connected through talking.

____ 2. Feel connected through sharing recreation/fun times together.

____ 3. Be touched non-sexually.

_____ 4. Having sex.

_____ 5. Receive verbal tenderness.

_____ 6. Receive physical tenderness.

_____ 7. Support my desire to live by the laws of man.

_____ 8. Support my desire to live by the laws of God.

_____ 9. Know that we'll stay together and feel secure in love.

_____ 10. Know we'll stay together and feel secure in finances.

_____ 11. Feel accepted and valued for who I am.

_____ 12. Feel accepted and valued for what I do.

_____ 13. Feel safe when I share who I am.

_____ 14. Be included in most decisions that affect my life or marriage.

_____ 15. Gain agreement and harmony in decision-making.

_____ 16. Know that he or she needs me.

_____ 17. Support my desire to give money away.

_____ 18. Support my desire to give gifts to others.

_____ 19. Support my desire to serve others.

_____ 20. Receive genuine appreciation of praise and affirmation.

_____ 21. Support my desire to have alone time.

_____ 22. Be physically attractive.

_____ 23. Be honest and trustworthy.

_____ 24. Support my desire to assist the younger generation in developing and leading useful lives.

_____ 25. Receive gifts.

_____ 26. Receive acts of service.

_____ 27. Develop with me a future plan for our marriage.

_____ 28. Develop complete faith in each other.

_____ 29. Become emotionally healthy.

_____ 30. Maintain a mutually vibrant spiritual relationship.

_____ 31. Apologize and seek forgiveness.

_____ 32. Resolve differences/conflicts/arguments.

_____ 33. Provide mutually satisfying communication.

_____ 34. Cope with crises and stress.

_____ 35. Understand my personality and gender differences.

_____ 36. Demonstrate a willingness to change (flexibility).

___ 37. Agree on how to raise our children.

___ 38. Be passionate and romantic.

___ 39. Socially connect with others.

___ 40. Maintain careful control over his or her expectations.

___ 41. Notice our positive relational history.

___ 42. Strive for mutuality and equality in our relationship.

___ 43. Share negative and positive feelings without delay.

___ 44. Accept my influence.

___ 45. Periodically update his or her knowledge of my greatest needs.

___ 46. Receive genuine appreciation for my service.

___ 47. Other need:

B. From the above list, pick your top ten needs in order of importance (e.g., #1 would be your most important need).

1. _____

2. _____

3. _____

4. _____

5. _____

6. _____

7. _____

8. _____

9. _____

10. _____

C. In order for your mate to completely understand your top ten relational needs, it's necessary to explain what each need means to you. For example, if one of your top needs is "provide mutually satisfying communication" then you will need to explain what that means. Moreover, if your mate was giving you "satisfying communication" then what would he or she be doing? Make your explanation as behaviorally specific as possible. In other words, tell your mate what specific behaviors he or she would be doing if he or she were providing mutually satisfying communication.

In the space below, define each top need.

1. _____

_____

2. _____

_____

3. _____

_____

4. _____

_____

5. _____

_____

6. _____

_____

7. _____

_____

8. _____

_____

9. _____

_____

10.

_____

_____

Now that you have discovered what your mate's needs are, we encourage you to spend at least twenty minutes per day this week "recharging" those needs. Ask your mate which relational need is the most important one for you to focus on this week. So you can remember, write down your mate's most important need in the space below. Refer to this page throughout the week so you will remember to concentrate on it.

Final Encouragement

1. Commit to reviewing these needs on a weekly basis with your mate. Ask if you are doing the things that will keep the marriage heading in the right direction.

2. In order to continue to reap the benefits of being in a support group and to maintain lasting change, we have found that it is very helpful to sign a marital commitment. This is one additional way to surround your relationship with accountability. Research studies have demonstrated that when someone signs their name to something, they are significantly more likely to maintain the commitment they signed. Take time to carefully read and sign the marital commitment on page 42.

3. Spend time each week reviewing the marital commitment so that you will keep doing the things that positively impact your marital relationship.

Marriage Commitment

I, _____ commit to doing the following six things on a daily basis to enrich my marital relationship:

1. To enter into the fourth and fifth levels of intimacy on a regular basis.
2. To recognize and avoid the four "germs" that can infect my relationship.
3. To place high value on my mate's personality. Furthermore, to strive for balance within my own personality.
4. To confer valuable distinction (honor) on my mate, marriage and family. Furthermore, to consider my loved ones' feelings and needs as just a little more valuable than my own.
5. To use LUV Talk in resolving any conflict or sensitive issue that could lead to any one of the "infectious" relational germs.
6. To spend at least twenty minutes per day "charging" my mate's most important relational needs.

_____   _____
Your Signature   Date

_____   _____
Mate's Signature   Date

Leader's guide

We recommend that you take this series and use it with small groups. We have provided a guide to help you. "A leader is the most important element in a group." Although this quote may intimidate some potential leaders, it is important to recognize that a group's success or failure depends upon the leader's ability to effectively lead. Our purpose for this section is to provide you with the information to successfully guide individuals into better, more satisfying relationships. We hope that you can move from possible intimation to excitement, as you recognize the key to leading is knowledge and skills. Over the next few pages, we will provide the knowledge and skills to be an effective leader of the *Secrets To Lasting Love* video series.

WHAT ARE THE QUALIFICATIONS OF AN EFFECTIVE SMALL GROUP LEADER?

1. Create a place of genuine commitment. We live in a world that is starved for meaningful relationships. People live across the street from each other for years and never know each other's names. Co-workers are just a voice on a telephone line half a continent away. Aunts, uncles and cousins are just names on a Christmas list.

People need commitment and a sense of community. They need to know they have a group of people who are dedicated to loving them, anxious to serve them, and willing to share the joys and sorrows of life with them. Your Secrets To Lasting Love group should be a place where people experience the joy of being committed to each other, and the sense of community and belonging that results from that.

In building commitment and community one of the most difficult things to keep a handle on is how everyone is feeling about himself and the small group process. Some people are vocal enough to let you know exactly where they stand, but most are shy about expressing their feelings about being in the group. It's good to remember that most people have ambivalent feelings about being in small groups. They are unsure if they'll fit in, if they

have anything worth contributing, if they will be treated with respect and dignity, and if they are genuinely liked and appreciated by other group members. If those issues aren't recognized and addressed early on, members can "dry up and blow away" without ever giving a hint they were in trouble. When that happens, everyone loses. The group isn't as strong because it loses the input of a unique, valuable person, and the person misses a chance to build relationships and strengthen his or her home.

People need to feel that they are a valuable part of the group. And while it is important for each person to make an effort to communicate value to the others, the leader can go a long way in setting the pace for that kind of appreciation and respect.

2 . Have an attitude of servant-hood. In other words, focus on the needs of the group and not your own. In order to do this it is important to ask them questions to draw out their needs. For example, "What will make this a great group experience for you?"; "What needs to happen to make this a '10' for you?"; or "What are your expectations for the group?" Questions like these can get to the heart of what people "need" from the group.

3 . Show a willingness to spend outside time with the group. Doing so is a tangible way of saying "I care about you."

4 . Commit to consistently communicate love and appreciation to the group as a whole and each member individually. Doing so will earn you a place of affection and respect with them forever.

5 . Take advantage of opportunities to praise the group members' strengths, talents and abilities in front of the others. In doing so, you model the very core of this program — HONOR.

6 . Maintain positive eye contact and good non-verbal communication with everyone in the room.

7 . Make a conscious effort to include everyone in group activities. This may take some gentle prodding on your part, but keep at it. It's good for the person and the group!

8 . Know the difference between persuading and forcing. Simply stated: Persuasion is the art of positive, motivational influence that prompts another person to respond in a "hoped-for" manner. On the other hand, force is a dominant, negative motivational influence that compels another to comply with an insisted-upon response. It targets a person's weakness and uses fear and guilt to motivate. Remember! Persuasion tends to build unity; force can tear unity apart.

9. Use humor appropriately. Remember two simple rules: (1) Be yourself, and use it to help effectively communicate key concepts to your group, not to simply entertain them. (2) Avoid using others' weaknesses or "slips" (like mispronunciations) to humor the group.

10. Model good listening skills. This primarily involves LUV Talk, a technique whereby you look for the issue behind the spoken words, restate what the other person has said, and lovingly confine your response to contribute to the best interest of your listener. Many times, people say one thing but mean something totally different. Good listeners don't always hear what is said verbally, but listen to "why" something was said or "what" was truly meant by the spoken words.

11. Communicate in a clear, simple interesting way. This simply means to speak with enthusiasm and energy and to say things as simply and directly as possible. Any personal experiences, (i.e., "the time we had a flat tire in the middle of the Mohave desert..."), can help keep the group's interest and attention.

12. Use emotional Word Pictures. An Emotional Word Picture is a communication method that uses either an object or a story that simultaneously activates a person's emotions and intellect. And it causes a person to not just hear our words but experience them. In using these, concentrate on the emotion you want the people to feel and design your picture around one of their interests. For example, in trying to communicate how excited you are when you're with your wife, you might say, "Being with my wife is so exciting, it's like walking into the world's largest mall and realizing that the entire mall is having a 99% off sale!"

13. Use the "Salt" principle. Salt makes people thirsty, and the goal of this principle is to create a thirst for constructive conversation in which both you and your group can learn about each other's needs. Put simply, it means to never communicate information you consider to be important without first creating a burning curiosity within the listener. For example, "This next concept is one of the most important things that I've learned. It has done more in my marital relationship than anything else." This type of statement forces others to thirst for the next concept you are referring to.

14. Use good discussion questions. A good question is one in which members discover truth for themselves. Therefore, don't ask questions that have one correct answer (e.g., "Is commitment important in a relationship?"). Furthermore, there are several different kinds of questions, each designed to elicit different information. Some of those types are:

* information and opinion, such as, "What do you think?"
* relational, such as, "How do you feel?"
* experiential, such as, "What was that like for you?
* Self disclosure, such as, "What's a fear you have?" and
* Accountability, such as, "How are you doing with your commitment to more fully honor each other?"

In order to ask good questions, we encourage you to think about some of these rules:
* Practice good listening skills. Ask questions to draw out someone's discussion.
* Encourage questions but stay focused on the theme. Postpone questions that don't apply to the session.
* Promote application to the principles. "How are things going with this area?"
* Promote transparency by being transparent as a leader.
* Promote the safety of trust and support. The group must support being confidential about personal areas.
* Be personal and caring. People respond to genuine caring.
* Encourage honesty but discourage a harsh spirit. Truth can be overwhelming if it is not shared in a genuine loving spirit.
* Look for ways to encourage each participant in their own personal growth.

The questions provided for you in this series have all been tested in groups going through this material. We think you'll find the majority of them helpful stimulants for discussion. However, we recognize that each group has its own personality. You may feel some of the questions listed will not be that helpful.

Occasionally, even the best of questions will backfire or fail to get a response. When that happens keep two things in mind: (1) It may be necessary to elaborate on what the question is asking. Restate it several times using different words and phrases. (2) Be prepared to "milk" your group members' responses to questions that don't seem to be generating as much of a response as you'd like. Essentially, "milking" an answer involves asking questions based on a person's response that will help him give you more information. For a more detailed explanation of this technique, see the book, *The Language of Love*, Focus on the Family, 1989.

15. Be aware of the different levels of communication and how they affect intimacy. There are several different kinds of communication, such as (1) Cliche conversation, "The weather has been hot hasn't it?" (2) Information and facts, "I'm going with a new firm next month." Or (3) Ideas and opinions, "I dislike what's going on with the homeless in our community." A simple rule of thumb here is that the greater the degree of risk in what's shared, the greater the potential for intimacy to develop.

16. Be Transparent. This can be a fearful thing for any leader, but the payoff is well worth it. As one veteran of small groups has put it, "What I lost in impressiveness, I gained double in approachability." With permission from your mate before the meeting, share your appropriate failures and struggles. The bottom line is: don't hesitate to use your own stories. *People get far more from a story than they do from content.* The best is when you use a story to convey content.

17. Manage conflict. For more information on this issue, see page 50-54.

18. Show respect for and sensitivity to each group member. Regardless of his or her background or faults, each person is valuable and has a unique contribution to make to the group.

19. Provide equal support and encouragement to each group member. Favoritism can hinder the group's ability to function. Be careful to be as impartial with each person as you can. Remember also that most positive change takes place in others' lives when they are encouraged, not discouraged or criticized.

20. Be genuinely enthusiastic. People love to follow someone who's excited about what he does. Allow the group to see your passion for helping them make their families a success, and watch your group take off.

21. Keep the group on schedule. There's a real art to this, because every group gets off track some time and there's nothing wrong with that. If you control things too rigidly, your group can become frustrated they're not being allowed to express themselves.

22. Keep discussions on the central subject while still allowing room for some digression. Some guidelines to follow are:

* Don't allow more talkative members of the group to ramble. Don't be afraid to interrupt and carry on.
* Permit those who are not as talkative more latitude in getting off the subject. What you lose in temporary continuity you gain in their long term input and involvement.

* Diffuse argumentation. If an argument or disagreement starts, don't allow it to continue. If you can reconcile the problem quickly, do so. Otherwise, defer it until after the session and meet with the parties involved.

* Use "steer 'em back statements" like, "That's an interesting point, Jim. Let's get back, though, to what we were saying a moment ago."

23. Be faithful to the leaders covenant. Almost nothing speaks as loudly to a group as its leader's integrity. Remember, they will see the covenant you sign and will be watching to see if you follow through.

24. Hold group members accountable to commitments made in the group covenant. This is, in some ways, the hardest thing to do in your group. All of us have a deep need to be liked, and asking tough questions like "Have you done this?" or "What's keeping you from completing the assignments?" can jeopardize our popularity. As tough as it is, remember that if you let your group "off the hook," you haven't done them any favors. Being committed to their best doesn't necessarily mean doing what's easiest.

WHAT ARE THE CHARACTERISTICS OF A SUCCESSFUL SMALL GROUP?

1. Bonding activities. Seek to build friendships outside of the meeting time whenever possible. Organize a meal or outing that is separate from your regular meetings.

2. Be a place of honest, open, loving communication. We've all experienced the discomfort of being in a group where the atmosphere was as thick as a San Francisco fog. More often than not, that kind of tension is created when communication breaks down. Honest, open communication is an atmosphere in which thoughts, ideas and feelings flow freely between members. It's characterized by a commitment to each other's value and a lack of fear of rejection. Specifically that involves a commitment to being a listener rather than a speaker. In other words, "It's more important that the other person express himself than it is for me to express myself."

3 . A commitment to handling disagreements in a healthy manner. This involves:

* The freedom to respectfully disagree with ideas, but the commitment to never attack people or their feelings. Much of this involves carefully selecting words that are positive and not negative.
* A commitment to react to disagreement with a spirit of inquiry, not defensiveness.
* A commitment to affirming and encouraging each other, rather than belittling.
* A commitment to accepting at least partial responsibility for misunderstandings.
* An understanding that each person's maturity level and life's experience gives him a unique and valuable outlook on life.
* A commitment to using non-verbal communication only as a tool to honor each other. (An angry look or a raised eyebrow can create mistrust and misunderstanding in the group. By the same token, a smile, nod or a pat on the back can be more powerful than words in creating closeness.)
* An understanding of the group's goals and thus issues that should or should not be addressed. It's important for every group to know subjects that are off limits. Do your best to keep the group off subjects like politics, current controversial issues or gossip about others.
* An atmosphere of freely given and freely accepted forgiveness. Nothing will shut down communication faster than anger and resentment. By making forgiveness an integral part of your group, negative feelings can be avoided and communication lines kept open.

4 . Safety and security. The group must be a place of emotional safety for everyone involved. When members know their successes, failures, doubts, struggles and fears will be met with understanding, support, encouragement and prayer, they're far more likely to be open and receptive to the group. Transparency without danger is a powerful combination for intimacy, change and growth. Furthermore, safety and security also means that members will keep what is shared in group confidential. In other words, confidentiality is the commitment not to disclose the content of any of your group meetings unless a person obtains permission.

5 . Be successful in reaching its goals. The old adage, "If you aim for nothing, you'll hit it every time," is certainly true for Secrets To Lasting Love groups. Poorly defined goals can lead to ambiguous results and ambivalent feelings of accomplishment for everyone involved. But, if goals have been clearly established and ground rules well laid, your group can feel good about what it has accomplished. By having a clear "measuring stick" of goals and expectations, members can take great joy in seeing how far they've progressed in their goal of making their homes places of honor. In the Secrets To Lasting Love program, we hope three goals can be achieved:

* A bond of love and commitment will exist between group members.
* Individual lesson goals will be accomplished.
* Each person's commitment to honor each other will grow.

If the majority of people in your group feel these goals have been met, they are likely to say the time and effort were well worth it.

6. Establish group rules. It is very important to establish some fundamental rules that will promote safety and security within the group. During the first session, brainstorm with the group which rules, if any, are needed. Some examples include:

* Respect time. Activities start and end on time.
* Open or closed group?
* Grow in fellowship with each other (willingness to share openly with group members).
* Confidentiality.

Be sure to write these rules down and remind members of their commitment to abide by these rules in the event that someone violates a rule. Remember, the purpose of the rules is not to form a rigid group, but instead, to form a sense of protection for group members.

DEALING WITH CONFLICT

Picture this stressful scene: Norma and I (Gary) can't wait to begin an evening session with our fellowship group. In the past months, we've grown close to everyone and meeting each week has been a highlight for both of us. Everyone is walking around, laughing, having dessert and catching up with each other about the past week's events. We've just settled into the comfort of our living room, ready for a great evening together sharing each other's lives.

Suddenly, the front door flies open and Bill walks in, fuming like an angry bull. He stomps across the room and takes a place on the couch. A few seconds later, Sally, his wife, walks in, her eyes red and puffy. She sheepishly moves to a chair across the room from Bill and sits down where she can be protected by the other wives.

I nervously open with prayer and then look at Bill. I feel like I'm sitting ten feet away from the mouth of Mount St. Helens. Thinking it might help relieve some of the tension, I begin by saying, "Well...uh...Bill...tell us how you're doing."

"Terrible!" he snarls.

"Okay," I reply, "tell us what's bothering you."

"If you really want to know," he says, leaning forward on the couch and looking me right in the eye, "I've been thinking about getting out of this group. No, in fact, I'll tell you what I've really been thinking about. I want out of my marriage! I can't stand that woman over there! I don't know if I can live with her another day!" His words rip through the air like daggers at a carnival show. I couldn't believe it. In two minutes, the evening had gone from easygoing to explosive. The peacefulness we'd all experienced just moments before had vaporized and left us all with our hearts in our throats. To make matters worse, not only were Bill and Sally at odds with each other, but so were the whole group! All the women instantly gathered around Sally and glared at Bill. The men, on the other hand, just looked at each other with, "Great...what do we do now?" written all over their faces.

I did what any normal, highly experienced small group leader would do. I panicked, and in what surely was the shortest group meeting in history I said, "Why don't we close in prayer?"

Conflict. If only we didn't have to live with it, but for right now, it's a fact of life. Conflict is as much a part of our existence as bills, laundry and love. For most of us, conflict is a word full of negative connotations: Anger, resentment, fear, hurt, worry and damaged or lost relationships. Yet, experts in small group dynamics say that successfully managed conflict is an effective key to a stronger group.

Thus, it's important to understand both the positive and negative effects of conflict and how you can manage it in order to make your Secrets To Lasting Love group stronger. Because, believe it or not, there are actually many benefits that come as you work through conflicts in a group.

Some of the benefits of conflict are:
* It can lead to a richer understanding of people and issues.
* It can stimulate member involvement and motivation.
* It can be fertile ground for ideas and new ways of doing things.
* Having experienced it together can give the group a greater sense of bonding with each other.

But there can also be negative effects of conflict:
* It can cause bad feelings between group members.
* It can lower group cohesiveness.
* It can eventually split a group apart.

Because conflict is such a volatile force, it's extremely important to know what it is and how to deal with it. At its heart, conflict is the polarization of two or more people over an issue or situation both are emotionally tied to and both feel threatened. Thus, in dealing with conflict it's important to deal both with issues and relationships. Successfully managed conflict puts a premium on both.

THREE KEYS TO SUCCESSFULLY MANAGE CONFLICT ARE:

1. Take control of the situation. This is one of those times when a more autocratic form of leadership is helpful. Your goal in doing so is not to stop the conflict, but to manage it successfully. In doing so remember:
* Allow frank discussion, but never let it degenerate to abusive discussion.
* Permit the group to interact with words of encouragement and insight, but do not let them choose sides.
* Don't allow on-the-spot diagnosis to take place. For example, "Bill, I think you're feeling this way because your heart isn't right."

2. Search for the cause of the conflict. Concentrate on the cause of the conflict, not the behavior involved. It's easy to become distracted by the symptoms of conflict, especially if things turn abusive or negative. However, like putting a Band-Aid on a bullet wound, the problem will never be solved until the cause of the behavior is dealt with. In dealing with its causes, it's helpful to know there are three major types of conflict, each originating from a different source:
* **Intrinsic conflict:** This type centers on issues whose source is in the attitudes and experiences each member brings to the group. It deals with differences in goals and priorities; different views on the meaning of Scripture; differences in the way people were raised or what they were taught as children; prejudice; guilt from unconfessed sin; and pain from unresolved conflict and hurts.
* **Interpersonal conflict:** It revolves around perceived differences between people. It deals with issues like status, power or authority; confusion about roles and/or responsibilities; personality clashes; and perceived inequities in the group regarding involvement, favoritism, commitment and trust.
* **Environmental conflict:** It finds its source in variable factors that are, generally speaking, beyond the control of individuals in the group. Fatigue, setting, weather and health are a few examples of this kind.

The best way to identify the type of conflict involved is to use questions that explore feelings and experience. "How are you feeling?" and, "Why are you feeling that way?" are two standard questions to use. In doing so, you help unmask what the real issues are. One of the most common avoidance techniques used by others when asked questions of this nature is

to answer a "why" question with a "what" response. For instance, if two men in the group are in conflict and one becomes angry you might ask him, "Why are you feeling that way?" A typical response would be, "Because he makes me angry!" While true, he's only told you what he's feeling, not why. So, be persistent. In using this technique, remember two important things:

* Anger is a secondary feeling rooted in something else, (fear, worry, anxiety, insecurity, etc.). So, unless it will cause more conflict, don't accept, "I'm angry," as an answer to "How are you feeling?"
* A person hasn't answered a feeling-oriented question until he or she has identified an emotion that uncovers an area of vulnerability. Again, unless it will make a bigger mess of things, continue to gently probe until he does so.

Conflict is a protective mechanism, so, usually, once a person has shared an area of vulnerability, it disarms the conflict. The issue is out on the table and can now be dealt with in a spirit of love, tenderness, compassion and understanding.

3 . Diffuse the conflict. This is done by discerning what the real issues involved are. The easiest to deal with is environmental, due both to its generally temporal nature and the fact that it generally centers on things and not people. Environmental conflict is usually mildly irritating rather than significantly problematic. So, relax and use humor if you can. ("Gosh, I thought that thing over there on the wall was a thermostat, not an oven dial!) Make the best of it and remember there's always next week!

At the heart of most interpersonal conflict is insecurity. For a variety of reasons, someone's significance and worth is usually threatened by what he or she perceives is going on with another person. The issue isn't really whether the perception is correct that someone is being favored, trusted more, has more authority, etc., but how the person feels about himself is the real issue.

Therefore, if power struggles, personality clashes and role confusion are taking place, gently probe the people involved with "how" and "why" questions that move them toward an acknowledgement that that's the cause.

If only two people are involved, an effective way to manage interpersonal conflict is to have them LUV Talk (session 5) with each other. In essence, this involves three steps:
* One person first listening to another;
* Then restating what the person has said until that person is satisfied the other person understands, and finally,
* Responding in a loving manner.

Make sure that the other group members remain silent during this process. Continue LUV Talking until each person is satisfied he or she has been heard. We have done this in group settings, and the modeling of conflict resolution is tremendous! We've seen times of genuine tension turn into a lesson on closeness in a short period. Then, whether you've asked the questions or had others quick-listen, ask for the group's help in giving encouragement, support and affirmation to the insecure person. In other words, involve the group in helping resolve those feelings of inadequacy. Remember, when insecurity is the issue, change in others won't solve the problem; affirming the worth of the insecure person(s) will.

Intrinsic conflict is rooted in either threatened convictions that create a fear of loss or in anxiety from unresolved past conflict. Experience is usually what helps shape those beliefs or creates the anxiety. If a woman in the group grew up with alcoholic parents, she may hold a strong conviction that to drink any alcohol is wrong. If someone in the group holds a different view, she may feel her conviction is being threatened and she's being pressured to do something that adversely affects her or others she cares about.

By the same token, a group member may have never dealt with the pain of living with a father who punished his children unnecessarily and was never satisfied with anything they did. So, that group member may strongly overreact to anyone who suggests he be more firm in disciplining his children for fear that the child would grow up in the same atmosphere of anxiety and fear in which he did.

The goal in unearthing the feelings behind intrinsic conflict is to simply understand, acknowledge and be sensitive to its source. Feelings that spawn intrinsic conflict are usually the most deeply rooted and personal. Because resolving most of these feelings goes beyond the design of the Secrets To Lasting Love program, the group sessions should be a place where members can find sympathy and understanding; however, they should be encouraged to seek outside help in coming to grips with resolving their past.

Thus, when dealing with intrinsic conflict issues, use "how" and "why" questions to uncover the issue and then move quickly to enlist the group's help in communicating understanding, sympathy, and prayer support. LUV Talking can also be used here.

If someone else feels she can be of particular help in resolving the problem, encourage her to meet with the hurting person outside the group. When it comes to intrinsic conflict, support and sympathize, but don't feel compelled to use group time to deal with all the issues involved.

Not that the support your Secrets To Lasting Love group can offer is not valuable. It's important to realize that support, sympathy and prayer can be an enormous first step

toward helping the person deal with the issues he or she is hurting from. Thus, it's not that Secrets To Lasting Love groups are designed to ignore needs for change, but that there are certain limits as to what can happen in the session itself.

ADDITIONAL GROUP LEADERSHIP ISSUES

1. *The Secrets To Lasting Love* video series is ideal for two to six couples. The group is small enough for everyone to feel comfortable discussing issues, yet large enough to offer diversity, different opinions and diverse learning methods. To launch the study, the host couple invites friends to join them in looking at an opportunity to change their marriages forever. Not everyone who attends the introductory session will become a part of the group, so invite a few more than will be expected to commit to the study. The host couple should be careful not to make false promises about the course, but make the evening a time of fun fellowship. Expectations should be clear. Many of the couples may not know one another, so spend time getting acquainted. This initial meeting will set the tone for the study. If you go over six couples then it should be called a "workshop" instead of a small group.

2. Set goals or develop clear group objectives. What are the member's expectations? It is crucial for group members to have a clear sense of the group's purpose and what are the expectations. Also, agree on an ending (e.g., meet for seven weeks, twelve weeks, etc.)

3. Never choose lecture over discussion. Prepare some of your own personal examples to promote discussion.

4. Prepare in advance by going through the video and material.

5. Determine how much time you have and how many questions you can discuss. We will mark (*) the questions that we feel are more vital. If you have additional time, then you could ask all the questions.

6. Prepare some practical ways that you plan to apply the principles you learned.

7. Help members remain solution-focused instead of problem-focused.

8 . Look for ways to draw out the shy personalities of the group. Don't let one person talk and control the discussion, including you the leader!

9 . Review the past week's and promote the next week's material. (Salt principle).

Is a Secrets To Lasting Love Small Group a challenge? Absolutely! But your commitment can make each member a vital, active part of your group.

Remember: ✳ Make it a place of honest, loving communication.
✳ Create a harbor of security for everyone there.
✳ Strive to make it a place of commitment and community.

Let everyone see its success. Then you will have participated in creating an experience that will affect others' lives for decades!

Have a great group experience!

Yours for richer relationships,

Dr. Gary Smalley   *Dr. Greg Smalley*   *Michael Smalley, M.A.*

SMALLEY RELATIONSHIP CENTER

Our mission is to create a marriage revival throughout the world by increasing marital satisfaction and reducing the divorce rate.

ENRICHMENT PRODUCTS

The Smalley Relationship Center has more than 50 marriage, parenting, and relational books, videos, and audio tapes to enrich all of your most important relationships.

SMALLEY ON-LINE

Our Web site provides weekly e-newsletters, new articles on marriage and parenting, interviews with authors, on-line enrichment through marriage and personality profiles. Preview or order our latest resources.

ENRICHMENT EVENTS

We offer events with nationally known speakers as well as our own speaking team. Events include nationwide Couples Conferences through satellite technology, special live conferences that focus on specific needs, workshops for continuing education, and much more!

COUNSELING SERVICES

INTENSIVE MARRIAGE COUNSELING — During the "intensive" you and your spouse will spend two days (Marriage Intensive) or four days (Couples Intensive) with our marriage specialists in Branson, Missouri. This concentrated time allows you to rapidly move down to the root of your problems in a way that traditional weekly therapy cannot duplicate. The Intensive programs have had remarkable success with couples in crisis.

PHONE COUNSELING — Are you having trouble finding a Christian counselor in your area? Do you want to work with a pastoral counselor who knows how to apply the teachings by the Smalleys? Phone counseling might be the perfect fit. Our trained counselors are standing by.

PROJECT SMALL GROUP

We are calling men and women to become "Marriage Champions" taking the step to becoming marriage small group leaders. On our web site we offer not only eight different series that you or your church can order but also support for leaders.

To contact us, call 800-848-6329
or visit www.smalleyonline.com

TAKE YOUR SMALL GROUP TO THE NEXT LEVEL

FOOD AND LOVE VIDEO SERIES

Improve your marriage while you improve your health with this new 4-tape video series, from best-selling author and speaker Gary Smalley. Learn how the quality of your relationships impact your health and how your health can impact your relationships in seven practical sessions. This enlightening series includes interviews of medical experts, professional psychologists and everyday people in a fresh documentary style format.

• Learn five relationship skills that can increase your immunity system by 500%.
• Learn to choose the right foods and how food affects our moods and self-image.
• Learn about the four relationship viruses that can kill our love for others...and much more.
Includes comprehensive study guide.

REAL LOVE IN THE REAL WORLD PUZZLE VIDEO SERIES

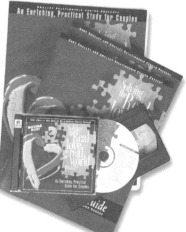

Today's world is fast-paced and hectic. Juggling jobs, kids, and hobbies is tough enough, but keeping a marriage alive at the same time..now that's a challenge. In this new 5-session series, members of the Smalley Relationship Center, including founder Gary Smalley, have embraced that challenge and offer a solution to this new world problem. This powerful, new, small group series is available as either a group study kit, complete with both VHS and DVD formats, study and leader's guides, and promotional kit, or, as a couples study—perfect for those couples wishing a private study.

KEYS TO LOVING RELATIONSHIPS

Over 1,000,000 homes and churches have watched this award winning series. "Hidden Keys," taught by Gary Smalley, includes 18 tapes on building successful relationships (each about 50 minutes). This series has no biblical references and makes a perfect series for churches and families to use as an outreach tool for secular audiences.

Keys To Loving Relationships Teaches: • How to recognize and value your mate's differences • The four essential elements every relationship needs • Overcoming anger—relationship's major destroyer • Word pictures—a communication method that increases intimacy and understanding • Becoming best friends with your mate and family • Discovering the value of your personality • Effective communication to create deeper intimacy...and much, much more! An invaluable, life-changing study for any small group.

*Tapes sold as sets or individually.

THE BEST-SELLING VIDEO SERIES IN AMERICA!

HOMES OF HONOR RELATIONSHIP SERIES I

This is the series that started it all. In Homes of Honor I, Gary Smalley, using his entertaining style, teaches couples how to reach the ultimate level of their relationship—honor. Over 4000 small groups around the country are using this series! This series is comprised of 4 video tapes with over 8 hours of teaching and includes a 110-page discussion workbook featuring a dedicated leader's section.

Topics include: The incredible worth of a woman • Discovering the value of your personality • The value of a man • How to resolve conflicts and anger • Finding fulfillment in knowing God personally.

HOMES OF HONOR RELATIONSHIP SERIES II

In this, the follow up to Homes of Honor I, Homes of Honor II, Gary takes couples even deeper into their understanding of relationships. This 8-hour series, taken from the "Keys to Loving Relationships" series by Gary Smalley, includes 9 topics with biblically based discussion sessions created specifically for small group discussion. Comes with 118-page study guide, including special leader's section.

Topics Include: Discovering and destroying the barrier to intimacy • How to change behavior and habits • How to encourage and energize your mate • How to divorce-proof your marriage • Discovering mutually satisfying sexual intimacy.

HOMES OF HONOR PARENTING SERIES

Parenting has never been an easy task, and going against the grain of today's popular views makes it even more difficult. Using the Homes of Honor Parenting Series, parents can discuss their strengths and weaknesses with other parents, gaining wisdom and insight. This insightful series has 8 sessions, with over 4 hours of teaching by Gary Smalley.

Topics include • What type of parent are you? • Discovering your child's personality type • Overcoming the major destroyer of families—a closed spirit • Providing loving support • Contracts, setting limits in a loving way • Powerful ways to motivate your children.